# LEARN CRICKET

## WITH

# *Geoff Boycott*

Stanley Paul
London

## Acknowledgments

The author acknowledges with thanks the help he has received from Terry Brindle, Sports Media Ltd, Art and Design Limited, Bill Ireland, Andrew Whittuck and Patrick Eagar in the preparation of this book.

This edition first published 1994

1  3  5  7  9  10  8  6  4  2

Copyright © Geoff Boycott 1976, 1994

Geoff Boycott has asserted the right under the Copyright, Designs and Patents Act, 1988 to be identified as the author of this work.

First published in the United Kingdom in 1994 by
Stanley Paul & Co Ltd
Random House, 20 Vauxhall Bridge Road, London SW1V 2SA

Random House Australia (Pty) Limited
20 Alfred Street, Milsons Point, Sydney,
New South Wales 2061, Australia

Random House New Zealand Limited
18 Poland Road, Glenfield, Auckland 10, New Zealand

Random House South Africa (Pty) Limited
PO Box 337, Bergvlei, South Africa

Random House UK Limited Reg. No. 954009

A CIP catalogue record for this book is available from the British Library

ISBN 0 09 177731 3

Design and page make up by Eric Drewery

Printed and bound in Great Britain by Richard Clay Ltd, Bungay, Suffolk

This book is based on *Geoff Boycott's Book for Young Cricketers* first published by Stanley Paul in 1976

# Contents

# Preface

This is John Arlott's original preface to *Learn Cricket with Geoff Boycott*, first published in 1976.

'Geoff Boycott in his great period was the finest batsman in the world; certainly the most dedicated. His batting bears the stamp of careful analysis and construction of method. His right hand is low on the bat, the left effectively high; the left does, positively, lead while the right provides the main propulsive force; and it is all done with quite unusually complete balance of power. His first movement is back and across. He is a careful assessor of the ball, with the great batsman's gift of rarely being in error as to whether to go forward or back. If his batting has one outstanding quality it must be that of quite meticulous placing; he plays through the gaps in a field with greater precision than any other contemporary batsman. The figures of Boycott's batting are convincing enough in themselves; they are even more impressive seen – as in fairness they should be – against the background of his isolation, of the stress and physical battery to which the target batsman is nowadays subjected.

At five feet ten inches, Boycott is of ideal height for a well-balanced batsman: he is firmly but not heavily built, a coherent mover, strong enough for his purpose and conscientiously fit. His batting is thought out, planned to make the most of his abilities while securing him as completely as possible against the perils to which all batsmen are heirs. He bases his technique on a defence organized as near to flawlessness as can be. Indeed, when he is in form he comes so close to ruling out error that it often seems as if he need never be out. He judges swing well, plays spin with genuine understanding and, despite the battering he has had, scores steadily against pace. At the start of an innings he plays himself in without anxiety, not the least worried if he does not score for half an hour while he takes the pace of the pitch and his measure of the bowling. Despite his quick assessment of the bowled ball, he often leaves his stroke quite late, yet without having to hurry it. Then he gradually exerts his range of strokes like a racing motorist opening the throttle and on his great days his batting has an air of inevitability. Geoff Boycott, a superb technician, has – as is well for the team he plays for – an unfailing hunger for batting, runs and success; and his successor is not in sight.'

John Arlott

# Introduction

Cricket is not an easy game. There are a few fortunate people who seem to take to it and do well without apparent effort but for most of us cricket demands a lot of practice and a willingness to work hard to maintain high standards.

If you want to get to the top or simply play to the best of your ability there is no substitute for practice. Not everyone is cut out to be a county player or reach Test standard but practically everyone who takes up the game can improve his or her performances by perfecting the basic techniques.

It's never too early to start. I went to a coaching school when I was nine and there have been many good players who started before that. If you can get professional coaching, that's the best way; if you can't there is a lot to be learned from watching good players.

Let me emphasize that I advise anyone to play sport rather than watch. It's nice to see youngsters at cricket matches and I think they should be made welcome, perhaps more welcome than they are at some places. But if you have a choice, be a player rather than a spectator.

When you do watch cricket watch the best players – and with your head as well as your eyes.

You will see they all have differences in style and approach but you may also be surprised how many similarities there are, how many basic·rules apply to them all. Ask yourself what a player does and why, see if you can spot the difference between one delivery and the next. If the captain makes a fielding change, see if you can spot the reason. In this way you will learn a great deal and enjoy the match all the more.

After all, enjoyment is what the game is all about. Because a professional cricketer earns his living from the game and has an additional responsibility to provide entertainment, he probably takes his pleasures more seriously than the man who plays purely for relaxation. So it should be.

But Sir Donald Bradman once said: 'If the game is not enjoyed, why bother to play it at all?' It took me a while to appreciate the value of that philosophy, but I recommend it to anyone.

Cricket can be something of an inconvenient game because it is time-consuming. Even cricket on the village green usually demands a full afternoon – unless, of course, somebody comes up with a demon bowling performance or one of the umpires has to catch an early bus. But the fact that cricketers are brought together for longish periods helps breed a unique sense of friendship and involvement – not just between team-mates but among rival teams.

This is certainly so in county cricket and local cricket has a special social atmosphere unlike any other game. It's a great way to spend your time.

I am often asked which of my performances have given me the most pleasure over the years and it's not an easy question to answer. Batting well on a difficult pitch for a modest-looking score can be as satisfying as hitting hundreds, but some achievements obviously do stick in the mind.

My first century for Yorkshire was especially sweet because it was scored in a Roses match when we were struggling a bit. The 1965 Gillette Cup final when I scored 146 and helped Brian Close put on 192 against Surrey will always rank high in my memory; then there was that wonderful tour of Australia in 1970-71 when we brought back the Ashes. I have mixed memories about that because I was injured, but it was a great tour.

My first match for England, being asked to captain Yorkshire, averaging 100 in a first-class season and scoring centuries against every other county and Test country – those are some of the other achievements which have given me pleasure over the years.

One thing is certain – nobody will ever achieve really good, consistent performances unless he masters the basics of the game. And the higher you go up cricket's ladder, the more important that becomes.

When I struggled to find form – and that happens to everyone at some time or another – I concentrated hard on getting the so-called simple things right. I was never afraid to go back to basics because that is where every good performance begins.

This book sets out to help you master the basic ingredients of cricket. I hope you find it interesting and helpful. Work hard at the game and it will repay you in many hours of enjoyment and a real sense of achievement. Believe me, it really is worth the effort.

Wherever I have used the male gender when referring to young cricketers, the comments of course apply to both boys and girls.

Geoff Boycott

# Batting

## GRIPPING THE BAT

It is important to have the correct grip to make sure that your hands work together.

Here is a good way to achieve this. Lay the bat face downwards on the ground and pick it up as if you were wielding an axe.

This should give you the natural grip with hands close together on the handle. The V's formed by the first finger and thumb of each hand will be on the same line halfway between the outside edge and the splice.

When you face the bowler make sure that the fingers and thumbs of both hands are well round the handle and the back of your left hand faces towards mid-off and extra cover.

## THE STANCE

Every batsman must feel comfortable at the wicket and have a relaxed and balanced stance. This is how I face the bowler.

See how my knees are slightly relaxed with my weight evenly balanced on the balls of both feet for quick and easy movement. My feet are roughly parallel, one on each side of the crease 4" to 6" apart. I find it comfortable to ground my bat just behind my right toes and rest my hands on my left thigh.

It is most important that the left shoulder should point at the bowler and the head should face down the pitch with eyes looking squarely at the ball.

*The beginning of every good innings. Comfortable, balanced and alert without being tense – a good stance has an air of authority about it, as Mike Atherton displays against the 1992 Pakistanis.*

# TAKING GUARD

I make sure the umpire gives me a guard from behind and over the bowler's wicket because this is the position from where he will adjudge me out L.B.W. or not out.

When asking for a guard hold your bat upright with its face to the umpire. In this way the umpire can see which stumps it is covering.

Many players ask for a guard 'from where the bowler bowls' – this makes no sense at all.

# THE BACK LIFT

A vital part of all batting strokes is the back lift. If you pick the bat up correctly it should go back towards first slip, then loop at the top before coming down straight.

The left arm and wrist do nearly all the work. Notice how my bat is taken back by my left hand and the face of the bat opens towards point.

Lifting the bat back is not natural and it requires hard work to get it right. I used to practise my back lift in front of a mirror and it has helped me to keep a straight bat.

# KEEP A STRAIGHT BAT

Most youngsters have difficulty in playing the ball with a straight bat. It is not easy and it requires a lot of hard work to get it right but this simple exercise helped me in my early days.

Drill a hole in a composition ball and thread some wire through it. Fasten the wire to a beam or a tree so that the ball hangs about waist high.

Then concentrate on hitting the ball steadily bringing the bat down straight. If you hit the ball correctly it will return to its original position for you to hit again and again. If it goes off at all angles you need more practice.

*Everything in line: Mike Atherton plays classically forward, bat straight – front knee slightly bent, head over the ball – to smother the spin of Mushtaq Ahmed.*

**13**

# PLAYING FORWARD DEFENSIVELY

Every batsman must learn to play forward and stop the good balls from getting him out. Learn to play forward correctly and you are halfway to becoming a good player.

Left shoulder and head lead towards the ball.

Left foot moving to the pitch of the ball.

Let the weight of your body come forward so that the left knee bends slightly and allows the heel of the right foot to ease off the ground. Then as you bring the bat down allow the right hand to relax its grip into the thumb and first two fingers. Look at the angle of the bat as the ball is met just in front of the left foot.

The left hand is always in control so that the ball is met with a straight bat.

Head over ball

# PLAYING BACK DEFENSIVELY

Having played the forward strokes you must learn to play off the back foot if you are to become a consistently successful batsman. All the great players move their right foot well back and across the stumps to bring the head in line with the ball.

Move right foot parallel to the crease to keep the body sideways on to the ball.

By keeping the left elbow high, it is easy to control the bat and allow the right hand to relax into a thumb and finger grip. I allow my right hand to slide down on to the shoulder of the bat for more control.

Note the angle of the bat.

Head over the ball

Finally – let the ball 'come on' to you and meet it with relaxed soft hands so that the ball drops down in front of you.

*A comfortable big stride, left elbow high, head over ball, weight transferred on to the front foot. Play this shot well and you are halfway to becoming a good player.*

# THE ON DRIVE

This is one of the most difficult strokes for young players to master. Make sure that you turn and dip your left shoulder towards mid-on. It will naturally follow that your left foot will open out so that the toes are pointing down the pitch!

Now watch as my left knee bends how the weight of my body is transferred onto my left foot and I hit the ball just inside my left toe.

Here with my left hand in full control I follow through with a straight bat towards mid-on.

# THE OFF DRIVE

The most important point about this shot is the movement of the left shoulder which should turn and point towards extra cover. By keeping your head close to the left shoulder, your eyes look down on the line of the ball.

Remember the wider the ball the more you turn your back on the bowler. In this way you make sure you stay sideways on and get your left foot to the pitch of the ball.

Now with the weight firmly on the left foot both arms follow through the line of the stroke.

# ATTACKING OFF THE BACK FOOT

It should be easy to hit an attacking back foot shot after learning to play back defensively. But young players find this the most difficult shot to play because they will try to hit the ball too hard. This means they throw the head back and scoop the ball up in the air.

Wrong

Be sure to make the most of your height by rising on the toes of your right foot as I do. Then with the left hand controlling the shot, punch at the ball with the right hand just before impact.

Force is not required – the power comes from timing.

Still keeping the head down let the bat follow through in the direction of the ball.

oing forward to off drive
gainst New Zealand in
978.

nd driving square
ff the back foot, a
troke in which
ontrol and timing
re more important
nan force.

# THE SQUARE CUT

When playing the square cut I pick the bat up high and take my right foot well back and across the stumps.

As this is basically a one-footed stroke, keep the weight firmly on the right foot with the toes facing point.

From this position fling the bat down and out to meet the ball. Remember it is essential to come down on the ball from above.

Now as I hit the ball my right knee bends slightly to allow my body weight to come forward into the stroke.

# THE LATE CUT

The late cut is a refinement of the square cut and is used to place the ball behind the stumps. There is a pronounced turn of the left shoulder and the right foot lands well back and across the stumps but pointing to third man.

I let the ball pass my body so that it is nearly level with the stumps before I meet it.

Then with a downward movement of the bat I delicately stroke the ball. Remember you are steering the ball – not hitting it. The pace of the ball will help it on its way.

# CUTTING OFF THE FRONT FOOT

To short balls wide of the off stump, young players should play this shot rather than the square cut. It is a natural 'cross' bat stroke and in junior cricket offers the best chance of hitting fours.

Put the left foot well forward with the weight of your body on that foot and throw the bat down and out at the ball with your arms at full stretch.

Always aim to hit the ball at the top of its rise and 'roll' your wrists over to keep the ball down.

bove left: *Javed Miandad*
*an suggest perpetual*
*lotion at the crease but*
*ere he is poised and*
*erfectly balanced on the*
*ack foot to play the*
*quare cut.*

bove right: *Neil*
*airbrother's game is*
*ased on finding gaps*
*the off-side field,*
*om the front or back*
*oot. Here, his weight*
*forward as he hits*
*quare.*

ight: *Whether*
*quare or late, Robin*
*mith of Hampshire*
*nd England is*
*mong the most*
*rolific cutters in*
*le game today.*

# THE SWEEP SHOT

To a well pitched up ball outside the leg stump the sweep shot is an effective way of scoring runs. Once you have mastered it you can disrupt any spin bowler's field.

When sweeping you must get your left foot on the line of the ball . . .

From this safe position hit down at the ball in a 'sweeping' motion.

So that even if you miss the ball it cannot spin back and hit your wicket.

Don't hit the ball too hard – just help it firmly on its way.

# THE PULL SHOT

When pulling the ball I try to get my right foot well back and outside the line of the ball.

Right foot points down the pitch.

With the weight on the right foot my left foot is carried away to open up my body 'chest on' and bring my head directly in line with the ball. Then I hit the ball at the full stretch of my arms . . .

. . . with the weight of my body carrying over on to the left foot. Again my right wrist has turned over to keep the ball down.

# THE HOOK

See here how my right foot has gone well back and across the stumps with my toe pointing down the pitch.

Now it is easy for me to hit through the ball making sure my right wrist turns over my left wrist to keep the ball down.

It's a great feeling to hook a ball to the boundary like this, but to play it with safety you must get into the correct position quickly.

In this way my body has opened up and my head is just outside the line of the ball.

The 'roll' of the wrist is essential otherwise the ball will go in the air for a catch.

20

*bove left: Neil Fairbrother is the most destructive one-day batsman in the world. Once
is front foot is inside the line of the ball, he can sweep the ball with contempt for any
eld placings.*

*bove right: Body 'chest on' to the ball, weight transferring from right to left foot as
lec Stewart pulls during his 190 at Edgbaston in 1992.*

*elow: I enjoyed that . . . hooking for four is always a great feeling. When the bowler is
ennis Lillee it is extra special.*

# THE LOFTED STRAIGHT DRIVE

When the average batsman tries to hit the ball 'over the top' he imagines he has to hit the ball very hard and scoop it in the air to clear the fielders. He is so anxious to see if he has cleared the fielders that he lifts his head before actually making contact with the ball and gives an easy catch.

**Wrong**

**Right**

The correct way is to hit firmly with your head down and eyes fixed on the ball. Do not check yourself while playing the shot. Hit down and through the ball in a flowing movement and let your arms – not your body – lift the ball over the fielders.

Now when you lift your head the ball should be well on its way to the boundary.

# MOVING OUT TO DRIVE

Whenever I get the chance I like to move down the pitch to drive a well-flighted slow ball.

My right foot then moves up just behind my left foot in a smooth gliding movement, with my head and left shoulder facing towards the ball.

I try not to move until the ball has left the bowler's hand and I have judged the flight correctly. Then with a high back lift I move my left foot one stride towards the ball.

And as my left leg goes out again to the pitch of the ball the weight of my body moves on to my left leg to allow me to complete my drive from a firm position.

# THE STRAIGHT DRIVE

If played correctly this is the safest and most rewarding shot in cricket because you are using a straight bat to hit the ball back past the bowler.

With my head and left shoulder pointing at the bowler my left leg goes out to the pitch of the ball.

Notice how my left foot points towards mid-off.

With my left arm in full control it is now easy to bring the bat down straight and hit through the ball. As I finish my shot notice how my bat and left arm are still pointing towards the bowler.

*A shot we do not see often enough – Australia's Dean Jones moving out to straight drive a spin bowler back over his head.*

# LEG GLANCE OFF THE FRONT FOOT

Sometimes it is difficult to hit the ball safely through the on side. When this happens the leg glance can be a great asset in keeping your score 'ticking over'.

To play it correctly you must get the left foot *inside* the line of the ball so that even if you miss the ball completely it will pass harmlessly down the leg side.

From this safe position turn the face of the bat at the moment of impact and deflect the ball to fine leg.

# LEG GLANCE OFF THE BACK FOOT

To play this stroke it is essential that the body opens a little and turns towards the ball. Therefore move the right leg well back and across the stumps with the foot pointing to mid-off.

Bring the left leg close to the right so that if the ball is missed it will hit the outside of the left pad . . .

. . . and at the moment of impact turn the bat face to deflect the ball. Remember – all the best players of this stroke let the ball come very close to them before they play it.

*A turn of the wrists at the right moment produces this most delicate shot.*

# THE FULL TOSS

Cricket crowds think any full toss is an easy ball to hit but so many batsmen get caught out off a high full toss, because it is almost impossible to get over the ball and hit it down.

When I receive a full toss above chest height I play safe and defend. I do not try to score off this ball despite the friendly advice from the crowd to 'hit it'!

If the ball is below chest height then I hit it for runs.

# HITTING A FULL TOSS

Most batsmen have strong right hands and feel much happier playing a cross bat shot but so often I see them get out to a full toss. Why? Because they let the ball come too near their body and hit at it with their arms bent.

I make sure I get my head on the line of the ball and the weight of my body on my left foot.

Then keeping my head still I can hit the ball well in front of my left leg with my arms at full stretch.

# YORKERS

Remember the ball is pitched near the batting crease so what usually happens when the batsman attempts to drive a yorker is that he swings over the top of the ball and gets bowled out.

Be content to jab your bat down on the ball to stop yourself from being bowled out. There will be plenty of other balls to hit for runs.

I've often heard stories of old time greats like W. G. Grace hitting yorkers for six! I've never seen this phenomenon happen and personally don't believe it is possible.

*Australia's David Boon shows how to deal with the well-delivered yorker at Kingston, Jamaica, in 1991.*

# DEALING WITH BOUNCERS

A bouncer is a difficult ball to deal with. However, if you keep your nerve then you shouldn't have too much to worry about.

Here a leg-side or straight bouncer – I duck inside the ball but turn my head and watch it over my left shoulder. I know I'm safe and I keep my bat well out of the way.

I deal with bouncers in two ways. It all depends on whether the ball comes down the leg-side or straight at me or alternatively if it comes down the off-side.

In both cases don't 'freeze' but do watch the ball closely and decide whether it is straight – leg-side – or on the off-side.

Now for an off stump bouncer I simply keep upright and sway back – no sense in ducking into it – again watching it whizz by.

# FACING FAST BOWLING

Young players often come up against bowling which is much faster than they are used to. You can see them instinctively back away from the ball and play the shot far too late.

When I play against a fast bowler I concentrate on picking my bat up early before the bowler delivers the ball . . .

. . . and by keeping a short back lift I gain extra time to play the shot.

28

here is more than one way
f dealing with a bouncer.
ec Stewart (above) ducks
neath one from Waqar
ounis, while Robin Smith
ght) sways away from the
e, never taking his eye off
e ball.

# DON'T AIM FOR SIX

Trying to hit sixes is a common fault of weekend cricketers. By trying to 'whack' the cover off the ball they lift their head and get caught out. Don't consciously attempt six hits. Concentrate on keeping your head down and hitting firmly through the ball.

Wrong

Right

As a professional I never set out to hit sixes. I aimed to time the ball well and I was sometimes pleasantly surprised when it went sailing over the boundary.

# BATTING IN WINDY CONDITIONS

Batting in gusty, windy conditions irritates all batsmen because it upsets their balance and makes it difficult to control the bat. When this happens it is impossible to hit the ball well.

Then by punching the ball firmly with only a short follow through – it is easier to retain my balance and time the ball correctly.

Faced with these conditions I find I keep better control of the bat by using a short back lift.

# BATTING ON A WET PITCH

Play back whenever possible to give yourself more time to watch the ball.

The last thing you want to do on a wet pitch is drive the ball off the front foot. The soggy turf makes the ball 'stop' and 'lift' so that you 'spoon' a catch to the fielders.

On a wet pitch any ball slightly under-pitched will tend to stand up and wait to be hit! So by staying back I have time to use the square cut, pull and hook shots which are safer and more effective in these wet conditions.

*Timing, not brute force, is the secret of a powerful stroke, as Graham Gooch shows.*

31

# LOSS OF FORM

All batsmen get out of form at some stage of the season and lose confidence in their ability to score runs. When this happens to me I go back to basics and cut out all the fancy shots.

Mid-on    Mid-off

I make myself play in the safety of the 'v' between mid-off and mid-on because all the shots in that area require a straight bat.

By keeping a straight bat I have more chance of middling the ball and less chance of getting out.

# PLAY YOURSELF IN

Sometimes batsmen get out because they try to play too many shots at the beginning of their innings. They do not give themselves time to get used to the conditions 'in the middle'.

Always hit the bad ball. But wait until your eyes get used to the light, the bowler's action and the pace of the ball off the pitch before you start playing all your shots.

I keep my score 'ticking over' with singles until I feel confident to play my shots.

# TWO SHOULDERED STANCE

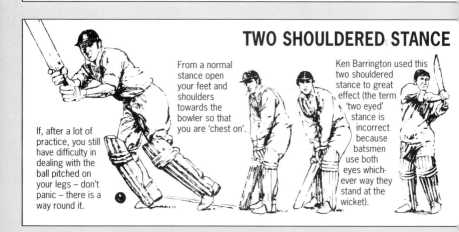

If, after a lot of practice, you still have difficulty in dealing with the ball pitched on your legs – don't panic – there is a way round it.

From a normal stance open your feet and shoulders towards the bowler so that you are 'chest on'.

Ken Barrington used this two shouldered stance to great effect (the term 'two eyed' stance is incorrect because batsmen use both eyes which-ever way they stand at the wicket).

*When form and confidence suffer the only way out is to start at the beginning and concentrate on playing with a straight bat. Better safe than out.*

# LEARN TO RELAX

My advice is to sit quietly and concentrate on the game. Watch the opposition bowlers and fielders for any points which may help you when you go out to bat.

Then when your turn comes you will find it easier because you have saved your energy and done your homework.

While waiting to go in to bat many players are so nervous and apprehensive that they fidget and chatter in the dressing room often taking little notice of the game in progress. This leaves them mentally and physically unprepared for batting.

# DON'T WASTE YOUR PRACTICE TIME

You shouldn't go to net practice and just slog away or laze around. Practise intelligently or you are wasting your time.

When you practise without anything specific in mind you can get into bad habits. I ask the bowlers to bowl so that I can improve or practise a particular shot which has been letting me down in matches. In this way I can improve my batting and enjoy my net practice.

# BATTING ONE HANDED

When gripping the bat with both hands many club cricketers have a tendency to let go of the bat with their weaker left hand. One of my favourite batting exercises is to practise hitting a ball with a bat in my left hand only. This improves my grip tremendously.

I drop the ball with my right hand and hit it into the practice net on the first bounce.

I force myself to grip the bat hard at impact because if I loosen my fingers I will hardly hit the ball.

See how I swing through the ball and finish in the correct position with my arm fully extended.

Concentration and a sense of purpose are important in the nets, where intelligent practice can help iron out problems. I have always enjoyed practice time in the nets and tried not to waste it.

## USE A LIGHTWEIGHT BAT

Occasionally a friend will ask me to try out his bat but I often find it is far too heavy for me.

A heavy bat is more difficult to control and without control it is impossible to time the ball correctly.

Timing is the secret of hitting the ball well. I use a light bat weighing 2lb 4oz and my advice to the average batsman is to use a lighter bat which is easier to control.

## CORRECT BAT SIZE

To bat well you must have the correct size bat. Many young players buy a bat which is too big for them thinking they will 'grow into it' and save themselves some money. This sort of thinking is wrong as it creates bad batting habits which may never be ironed out in later years.

The best way to find the right size bat is to take up your normal stance. The bat should rest behind your right toes – not away from your feet – with the top of the bat handle resting against your left thigh.

If the bat handle rests above the crotch – then the bat is too big for you.

If it is essential to save money, then buy a small bat. Remember, even Sir Leonard Hutton, one of the all time greats, used a Harrow size bat.

## CHOOSING YOUR OWN BAT

Many cricketers ask me how to choose a bat. My advice is to take great care in selecting your bat for 'feel' and balance.

I choose my bat by picking it up and playing a few 'fresh air' shots until I find one which 'picks up' easily and I feel happy with. A well balanced bat should lift easily and feel an extension of your left arm.

Remember no one else can choose your bat for you – buy the one which *you* 'feel' is right.

Equipment is something for personal taste, but to international players like Graham Gooch and Mike Atherton, it is second nature to be properly kitted out in every way. Remember, a bat on the small or light side is less of a disadvantage than one which is too big or heavy.

# ARE DIRTY BATS LUCKY?

I cannot understand any batsman putting his bat away without cleaning it first. After all, a good workman should look after his tools.

Yet I have seen some Test players afraid to rub the ball marks off their bats. Superstition? It would seem so! They believe that their run of good scores would come to an end by cleaning the blade.

This superstition is not for me and I clean my bat with fine sand paper after every innings.

# NEW GRIPS FOR OLD

A friend will sometimes ask me to try out his bat but usually I can hardly hold it because the rubber grip is so slippery.

Very few club cricketers bother about the rubber grips on their bats but I'd hate to think how many runs this costs them each season. Change the rubber grip at the first sign of your hands slipping.

Make sure you use some strong clear glue to make the rubber stick firmly to the bat handle. This will stop the rubber grip revolving round in your hands.

# A BATSMAN'S EQUIPMENT

You may think this is a lot of equipment for one batsman but this is what I wear and it helps me to bat with confidence.

Whether practising in the nets or playing in a match, always wear pads, gloves, a protector and thigh pads. Remember a cricket ball can be a hard and painful object if you are at the receiving end! This equipment could save you from severe bruising or a crippling injury.

Protector
Thigh Pad
Gloves
Pads

*Oh dear! Perhaps Tim Curtis, seen here batting for Worcestershire against MCC, is one of those with a superstition about cleaning a 'lucky' bat.*

# Bowling

With a new ball and a good bowling action any young person can learn to make the ball swing in the air and move in or out off the seam – provided he or she learns to grip the ball correctly.

A young bowler must decide whether to bowl out-swing or in-swing and set the field accordingly. Both types of swing require different field settings so don't try to bowl both in the same over until you have got control of swing, length and direction – otherwise your bowling may prove expensive and involve risks to your close-in fielders.

Except where indicated, all the grips in this section are for right-hand bowlers. For left-hand bowlers read 'left' for 'right'.

Note – when the new ball starts to lose its gloss, it is vital that all types of bowlers work hard at keeping one side polished and shiny by using sweat and/or saliva.

## The grip for right-arm out-swing

Point the seam of the ball towards the slips and place your first and second fingers on either side of the seam. Your third and fourth fingers should curve naturally down the side of the ball while your thumb rests on the seam underneath the ball.

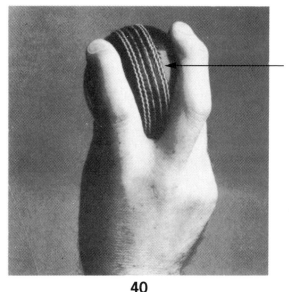

polished side on the right

## The grip for right-arm in-swing

Point the seam of the ball towards fine leg and place your first and second fingers on either side of the seam. Your second finger should lie parallel to the seam while the ball of your thumb rests on the seam underneath the ball. Let your third and fourth fingers curve naturally down the side of the ball.

polished side on the left

## Spin bowling

Although all bowlers need to concentrate on bowling good length and direction it is more important for budding spin bowlers to learn to spin the ball *first*. Experiment and then decide whether you want to be an off-spinner or a leg-spinner because it is difficult to bowl both breaks and impossible to set attacking fields for a bowler bowling both types of spin in the same over.

## Leg-spin

Space your first and second fingers comfortably apart *across* the seam with the top finger joints taking most of the pressure.

Your third and little fingers are naturally below them with the top joint of your third finger lying along the seam and pressing hard up against it.

Keep your wrist cocked inward and as you deliver the ball flick outward and upward with the third finger to impose spin. The action is similar to turning a door knob from right to left.

# Off-spin

Grip the ball so that your first finger lies along the seam with the top joint slightly bent and biting into the near edge. This is the main finger which imparts spin.

Your second finger should be spaced comfortably but well away from the first with the other two fingers curled naturally underneath the ball. Your thumb will rest on the other side of the ball near the seam. To spin the ball rotate your hand clockwise much the same as turning the knob to open a door.

## Slow left-arm

The grip for the left-arm orthodox slow or slow medium bowler is the same as for the right-arm off-spin bowler, except in reverse, so to speak. Follow the instructions given for the off-spin grip. But note that your hand will rotate in an anti-clockwise direction.

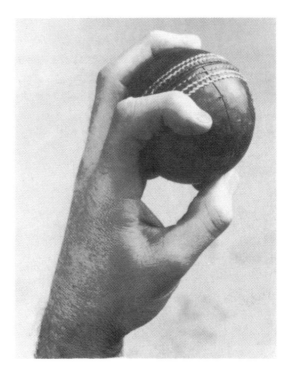

Opposite: *Three varieties of spin bowling, but they share the common call for accuracy, control and variety. Phil Tufnell (top left), England's star left-arm bowler; Mushtaq Ahmed (top right), the Pakistani leg-spinner; and the Australian off-spinner, Tim May.*

# BASIC BOWLING ACTION 1

A good bowling action is essential, so watch the bowler.
His run up is smooth and relaxed as he walks the first pace or two then gradually increases his speed so that only in his last few strides does he reach his full momentum.

In the last but one stride he springs off his left foot and turns his body sideways allowing his right foot to pass in front of the left.

As his right foot lands just behind and parallel to the crease his body is now sideways on to the batsman and he is looking down the pitch from behind his extended left arm.

# BASIC BOWLING ACTION 2

In the delivery stride the bowler's body swings forward with the left arm thrown towards the batsman and the right arm coming upwards rather like a cartwheel.

To help keep his body in a sideways position his left foot lands pointing to fine leg and directly in line with the right foot. The weight of his body is now firmly on his left leg and his arm is high and ready to deliver the ball.

Once he has released the ball his right arm is carried down and across his left thigh while the left arm swings well back out of the way. He continues to follow through for a few paces to keep his rhythm.

# GREAT BOWLERS USE THEIR HEADS

Many people think bowling is just a physical exercise and that bowlers run up to bowl without 'thinking'. All the great bowlers concentrate just as hard as a batsman.

As the bowler walks back to his bowling mark you can see him rubbing a shine on the ball. But all the while he is thinking out what kind of delivery he should bowl next.

(Thinks) This time I will bowl him a bouncer.

Before starting his run up he has a clear picture of what ball he intends to bowl so that during his 'run in' he can watch the batsman and concentrate on the spot where he intends to pitch the ball.

Generating speed and accuracy is not just a matter of racing to the wicket and throwing yourself into a delivery. A good bowling action is progressive and controlled, as shown by Curtly Ambrose (above) of West Indies, and (right) the Pakistan left-armer Wasim Akram.

# BOWLING FOR BEGINNERS

Bowling is not a natural action like throwing, but all youngsters can learn to bowl well enough to enjoy themselves if they follow this simple exercise.

Stand with your feet astride and arms sideways. Then rock from one foot to the other keeping your arms outstretched.

Continue rocking with your arms swinging loosely like the sails of a windmill.

Now do this with the ball in your hand and after rocking a few times, let the ball go. You are now bowling.

# LEARN TO BOWL STRAIGHT

The first essential is to hold the ball with your fingers and not in the palm of your hand.

If you want to be a fast bowler you can model yourself on one of the great Test bowlers.

Secondly, you will have to learn to bowl straight and to do this you must look down the pitch from behind your left arm and shoulder.

Try this simple practice: Chalk some wickets on a wall, mark the crease line and an aiming target in front of the stumps. Then, bowling with a rubber ball, concentrate on hitting the target over and over again.

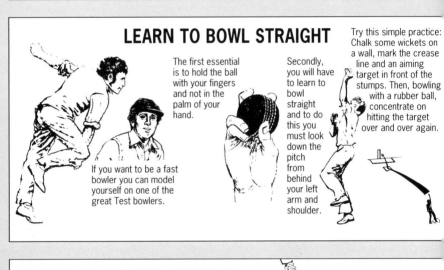

# DON'T WASTE THE NEW BALL

It is a bowling 'crime' to waste the new ball by bowling wide of the stumps so that the batsman does not have to play a shot.

When I open an innings I am delighted if I don't have to play the new ball much in the first few overs. It gives me a chance to settle down and get used to the conditions while the shine is going off the ball and the bowler tires – all to no purpose.

At the start of an innings the advantage lies with the new ball bowler – not the batsman. The bowler must retain his advantage by bowling straight enough to make the batsman play.

*Accuracy is the fundamental priority of every bowler, and few are consistently straighter than Pakistan's pace-bowling phenomenon Waqar Younis – hence, his unusually high percentage of dismissals bowled or L.B.W.*

# BOWLING AGAINST THE WIND

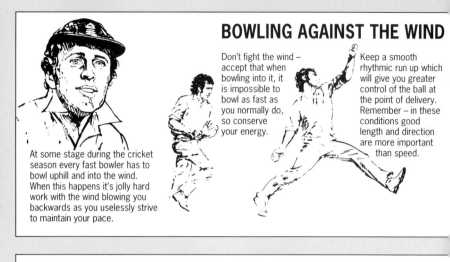

At some stage during the cricket season every fast bowler has to bowl uphill and into the wind. When this happens it's jolly hard work with the wind blowing you backwards as you uselessly strive to maintain your pace.

Don't fight the wind – accept that when bowling into it, it is impossible to bowl as fast as you normally do, so conserve your energy.

Keep a smooth rhythmic run up which will give you greater control of the ball at the point of delivery. Remember – in these conditions good length and direction are more important than speed.

# BOWLING AT TALL MEN

Once you can bowl good length balls you must learn to vary your length according to the batsman.

When bowling to a tall batsman an ordinary length ball becomes a half volley and is hit for four. His extra height means he has an enormously long stride and he gets nearer to the pitch of the ball than most batsmen.

In this situation you must make it difficult for the tall batsman to score runs by shortening your length and under pitching considerably.

# EXPERIMENT IN THE NETS

At net practice batsmen tend to think bowlers are only there to help them improve their batting. They couldn't be more wrong!

Watch the England bowlers at the nets. They spend the time trying out variations to add to their bowling armoury. Next time you go to practise, experiment. Try something new by attempting to bowl a yorker, a slower ball, a bouncer, or even try bowling round the wicket.

In the nets many bowlers often bowl at one stump to help them achieve greater accuracy.

For a batsman, the advantage of height is being able to turn good-length balls into half volleys. Australia's Tom Moody demonstrates his reach.

# Fielding

## CLOSE-IN FIELDING

When fielding close to the wicket it is important to stand so that you can sight the ball and move quickly in any direction. So make sure your legs are comfortably apart with your weight evenly distributed on the balls of both feet.

Both knees should be bent to keep the seat well down and the hands should be relaxed in front of and between the knees.

Here are some golden rules to help you take great catches:

1. Concentrate hard.
2. Expect every ball to come to you.
3. Don't move until you have sighted the ball off the bat.

## STOPPING THE BALL

When fielding, the first job is to stop the ball with your hands, but if that fails, with some other part of your body. To make sure of doing this you must get your body behind the line of the ball in either of the following ways.

Meet the ball chest on with your heels together and toes apart. Bend your knees to allow the body to get well down and receive the ball in front of your feet with the fingers pointing down.

Many professional cricketers, myself included, prefer to meet the ball sideways on. By dropping onto my left knee and opening up my right foot my body presents the maximum barrier to the oncoming ball. My hands receive the ball in front of my left thigh.

*They can come at all heights and angles when you field in the slips. Graeme Hick demonstrates how concentration, alertness, and the ability to watch the ball, lead to catching most of the chances offered.*

# ATTACKING FIELDING – THE PICK-UP

When you can stop the ball, learn how to save runs by attacking fielding. Always watch the batsman – not the bowler – and as the ball is bowled walk in slowly so that you can accelerate in any direction to meet the ball.

Now watch me. As I reach the ball my body turns sideways so that my right foot in its final stride lands at right angles to the line of the ball.

With the weight firmly on my right foot my hands move down to receive the ball just in front of my right toe. I never take my eyes off the ball until it is safely in my hands.

# ATTACKING FIELDING – THE THROW-IN

Once I receive the ball in the attacking fielding position my body is naturally placed for aiming a fast 'throw-in'.

So from here I take my right arm – with wrist cocked – straight back until it is in line with my right shoulder and at the same time point my left arm straight at the target. By using the left arm as an aiming device I can achieve greater accuracy and lessen the chance of making a 'wild throw'

As I throw the ball the weight of my body automatically transfers onto my left foot and with the ball speeding on its way my right arm is pointing down the line of flight.

*Robin Smith has made himself one of the best outfielders in the world through sheer hard work. He is quick to the ball, smooth of pick-up and accurate of throw.*

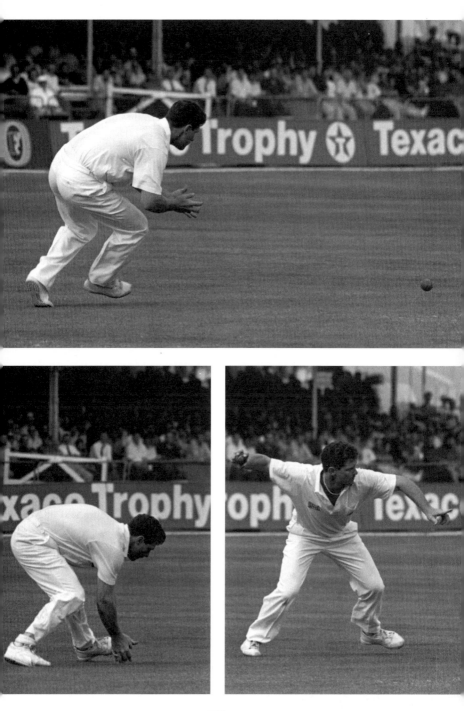

Young cricketers when faced with this situation are frightened to catch the ball for fear of being hurt, but if you follow these simple instructions you have nothing to worry about.

# HIGH CATCHES

Spread your hands and fingers in a wide relaxed web and catch the ball at the base of the fingers.

1. Don't move until you have sighted the ball then get under it quickly.
2. Once there, keep your head still and watch the ball.
3. Then raise your hands early enough to catch the ball at about eye level.

As the fingers close round the ball let the hands 'give' towards the chest. This cushions the impact of the ball and stops it from bouncing out of your hands.

# GIVE YOURSELF ROOM

I'm not surprised this young man dropped the ball. It came at him straight and fast like a bullet and he got his hands to the ball all right – but out it bounced! By standing still and trying to catch it in front of his body his hands had no room to 'give' with the ball.

When faced with this situation I move my body slightly to one side of the oncoming ball . . .

. . . so that as I take the catch my hands have room to 'ride with the ball'. This cushions the impact and stops it from bouncing out of my hands.

# CATCHING A HARD ONE

Now as your fingers close round the ball you have room to let your hands 'ride with it' towards your shoulder. If you meet the ball with rigid hands it will bounce out.

I think the most difficult catch to take is when the ball is hit hard and flat and coming straight for your head as it is impossible to catch the ball in the normal way.

When taking this catch make a 'web' of your hands with the fingers pointing upwards then move your head slightly to one side – still keeping your eyes on the ball.

*above: Balance and reflexes personified as Graham Gooch stretches to take a one-handed catch at third slip, Gus Logie the unlucky batsman.*

*right: Take no chances — eyes on the ball, hands high and poised, legs braced. Graeme Hick shows how to take the sort of skier which always looks easier than it is.*

# PRACTICE AT PLAYTIME

You can always improve your 'ball sense' if you are keen enough. Here is a simple example of how to improve your catching and throwing.

If you are at a loose end on your own, chalk a target on a wall, stand a few yards away and throw a rubber ball at the target – catching it as it bounces back.

If you have a friend willing to play with you stand a few yards apart facing the wall. Using the same target throw and catch the ball in turn.

To improve your slip fielding and quicken your reactions try this game. Two people face a wall at a distance of some 4 to 6 yards. A third person stands behind them and throws a rubber ball at the wall. The two people facing the wall have to sight and catch the ball on the rebound.

---

# FIELDING CAN BE FUN

Fielding is the easiest and most natural of all cricket activities. But you can't call yourself a cricketer until you are a good fielder.

Have a bit of fielding practice in front of the pavilion before the start of every match. Even Test cricketers have a few minutes warm up before they take the field. It gives them a chance to get the feel of the ball.

When your team takes the field don't treat it as a chore – go out meaning to enjoy yourself. Good fielding will inspire your team and help the bowlers by saving runs and creating a run out.

---

# CRICKET FOR EVERYBODY

You often see a game of cricket between youngsters with one or two talented players doing all the batting and bowling. Those who do nothing but field soon get bored and drift away from the game into some other activity. Here is a game of cricket which gives everyone an equal chance at batting, bowling, wicket-keeping and fielding. Spread out in these positions.

Each batsman receives two overs then everyone changes round clockwise: wicket-keeper 8, to batsman 1, to square leg 2, to mid-on 3, to bowler 4, etc.

By continuing in this way everyone is kept interested and enjoys the game.

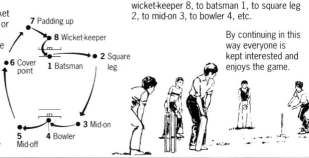

7 Padding up
8 Wicket-keeper
6 Cover point
1 Batsman
2 Square leg
3 Mid-on
4 Bowler
5 Mid-off

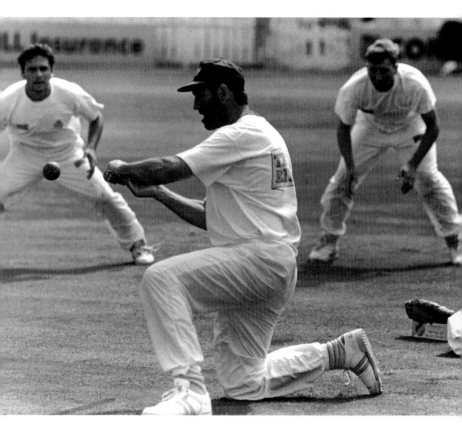

Slip catching practice has become an ever more important part of every team's preparations. Here, Graham Gooch shows one method, with Mark Ramprakash and Mike Atherton filling the slip positions.

# Captaincy

Captaincy has been described as a gift, an acquired skill, an art and a science, but whichever way you look at it, captaincy plays an important and sometimes vital role in cricket.

When a side wins a captain is not usually given special credit; if a side loses it is not uncommon for the captain to be blamed. Human nature being what it is nobody wants to admit to playing badly, so everybody tends to look for a scapegoat – and the captain can come under fire from batsmen, bowlers and fielders alike. Even spectators usually reckon they could have done a better job, so don't expect too much credit for your efforts.

Because of this there may be a tendency to try to please everybody – but resist it. Too much well-meaning advice from your players and outsiders can only complicate matters for you. If you are going to take responsibility for decisions do yourself justice by making them yourself. In other words, have the courage of your convictions.

That does not mean you cannot benefit from the experience and knowledge of others. When you feel it necessary, confer with your vice-captain and accept a little help from your players. You are always learning at this game and a captain has to be willing to learn faster and more often than any of his players. But a captain has to be positive and decisive, even when there are half a dozen awkward factors which have to be weighed in his decision.

If you don't always feel absolutely certain that your decision is right – and that is bound to happen if you are honest with yourself – at least look and act in a positive fashion. Keep a cool head, don't get ruffled or show you are worried and above all don't change your mind with every delivery or the team will soon become uncertain and lose confidence in you.

On the other hand a captain has to be flexible, to keep an open mind and try to suit his tactics to a game that can change by the minute. It is not a crime to change your mind, provided that you

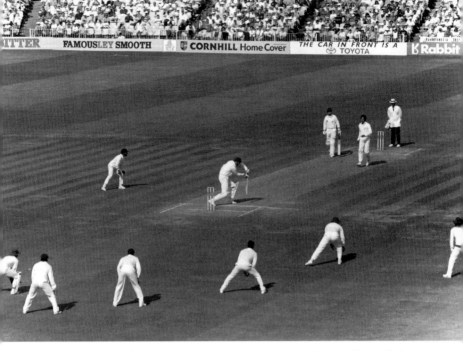

*On the attack! Wasim Akram has seven men in close catching positions during the 1992 Oval Test.*

think changes through and don't make them in an atmosphere of panic.

Always give encouragement when you feel it is due, although sooner or later you will have to be critical of the team and individual performances. That is inevitable and an important part of any captain's responsibilities.

Try to be constructive in your criticism, remembering that individuals are likely to react in different ways. Don't be afraid to be forceful when a point has to be made but guard against the kind of criticism which makes a player feel resentful.

Study the personalities of your own team as closely as you study the opposition's strengths and weaknesses. Your technical ability as a captain is entirely a matter of your own performance and experience but you can become a really good leader if you discover how to make a team work together.

It's a difficult job for which there is no easy formula, no straightforward method which any textbook can teach. It's very much up to you.

# Field setting

## Out-swing, right-arm

(a) Good pitch

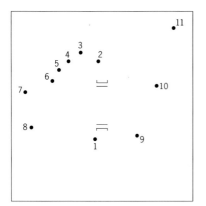

(b) Slow or wet pitch, with the occasional ball 'stopping'

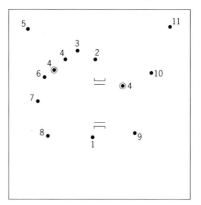

| (a) | (b) |
|---|---|
| 1. Bowler | 1. Bowler |
| 2. Wicket-keeper | 2. Wicket-keeper |
| 3. First slip | 3. First slip |
| 4. Second slip | 4. Second slip would stay there or move to second gully or short square leg depending on the wishes of the bowler |
| 5. Third slip | 5. Third man |
| 6. Gully | 6. Gully |
| 7. Square cover point | 7. Square cover would move to a more orthodox cover position in front of the wicket |
| 8. Wide mid-off – more or less extra cover | 8. Mid-off would move straight |
| 9. Mid-on | 9. Mid-on |
| 10. Square leg | 10. Square leg to backward short leg to catch the occasional ball which 'stops' or 'pops' |
| 11. Fine leg | 11. Fine leg |

# In-swing, right-arm

(a) Good pitch

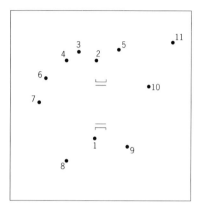

1. Bowler
2. Wicket-keeper
3. First slip
4. Second slip
5. Leg slip
6. Gully
7. Cover point in front of square
8. Straight mid-off
9. Mid-on
10. Square leg
11. Fine leg wide of leg slip

(b) Slow or wet pitch, with the occasional ball 'stopping'

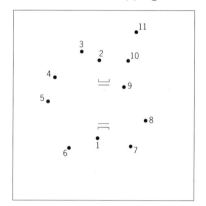

1. Bowler
2. Wicket-keeper
3. First slip
4. Gully
5. Cover point in front of square
6. Straight mid-off
7. Mid-on
8. Mid-wicket
9. Slip would go to short square leg
10. Leg slip would go square or wider
   Both to catch the ball which lifts off a length
11. Fine leg would move finer or 'inside' the leg gully

**63**

# Left-arm swing bowling over the wicket

(a) Good pitch – new ball, attacking field

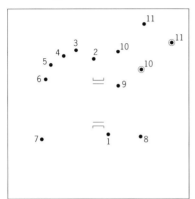

(b) Slow or wet pitch – occasional ball 'stopping'

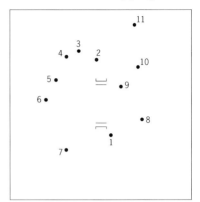

1. Bowler
2. Wicket-keeper
3. First slip
4. Second slip
5. Wide third slip
6. Gully
7. Extra cover or wide mid-off saving the single
8. Wide mid-on or straightish mid-wicket saving the single
9. Short square leg
10. Leg slip – vary position
11. Fine leg outside leg slip or inside wide leg gully

1. Bowler
2. Wicket-keeper
3. First slip
4. Second slip
5. Gully
6. Cover
7. Extra cover moves straighter to mid-off
8. Wide mid-on or straightish mid-wicket saving the single
9. Square leg to short square leg
10. Leg slip moves squarer or wider
11. Fine leg moves finer or 'inside' the leg slip

# Off-spin, right arm

(a) Good pitch

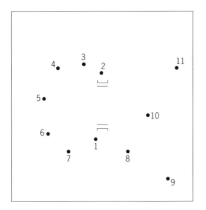

1. Bowler
2. Wicket-keeper
3. Slip
4. Short third man saving a single
5. Cover point
6. Extra cover
7. Mid-off
8. Mid-on
9. Deep mid-wicket – straight
10. Mid-wicket
11. Backward square leg saving a single or on boundary

# Off-spin

(b) Spinning pitch – attacking field

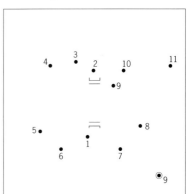

1. Bowler
2. Wicket-keeper
3. Slip
4. Short third man saving a single
5. Extra cover
6. Mid-off
7. Mid-on
8. Straight mid-wicket
9. Forward short leg should crowd the new batsman but once the batsman starts hitting out I suggest he be removed to deep mid-wicket
10. Leg gully
11. Backward square leg on boundary

## Leg break, right arm

(a) Good pitch

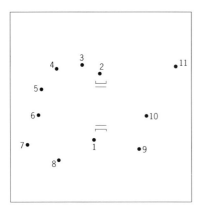

1. Bowler
2. Wicket-keeper
3. Slip
4. Short third man saving a single
5. Squarish cover point
6. Extra cover saving a single
7. Deepish extra cover
8. Mid-off not too near
9. Mid-on
10. Mid-wicket
11. Deep square leg behind square

## Leg break

(b) Slow pitch, 'turning a bit'

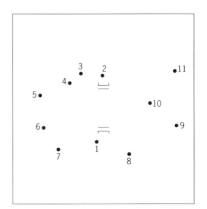

1. Bowler
2. Wicket-keeper
3. Slip – wider ⎤ Both slightly
4. Short third ⎬ nearer than on
   man to gully ⎦ a good pitch
5. Squarish cover point
6. Extra cover saving a single
7. Mid-off now saving the single
8. Mid-on
9. Deep mid-wicket
10. Mid-wicket
11. Deep square leg just behind square

# Left arm slow bowling around the wicket

(a) Good pitch

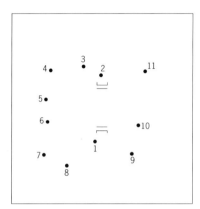

(b) 'Turning' pitch – attacking field

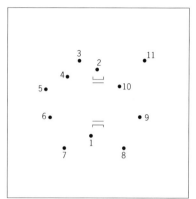

1. Bowler
2. Wicket-keeper
3. Slip
4. Short third man saving a single
5. Cover
6. Extra cover
7. Deepish extra cover
8. Mid-off
9. Mid-on
10. Straightish mid-wicket
11. Short fine leg saving a single

1. Bowler
2. Wicket-keeper
3. Slip
4. Gully
5. Square cover
6. Extra cover
7. Mid-off
8. Mid-on
9. Straightish mid-wicket
10. Short square leg
11. Saving a single behind square leg

# Wicket-keeping

Alan Knott, one of the best and most experienced wicket-keepers in the world, said: 'Wicket-keeping is hard work but wonderfully rewarding because you are never out of the game.'

There are two chief essentials for keeping wicket – an ability to sight the ball early and then to catch it, whether it comes from a ball bowled, a hit or a throw-in.

On taking the ball you must 'give' a little with the hands, reducing resistance and the risk of the ball jumping out of the gloves. This 'give' also helps prevent bruising. Relax your hands and try not to keep the fingers rigid; they should form a padded cup into which the ball will sink.

Dismiss from your mind any thought that the ball is going to hit the wicket, the batsman's body or even go for runs, and build up your powers of concentration to the point where you believe and expect every ball is coming through to you.

## Equipment

The most important part of any wicket-keeper's equipment is obviously his gloves, and the choice is a matter of personal preference. Some keepers like a supple pair with hardly any cushioning so that they feel the ball as much as possible; others prefer a heavy, well-padded pair for protection. Use the ones with which you feel happy and comfortable.

Whichever you choose I advise all youngsters to use a pair of cotton or chamois inners. Dampen them to make them pliable but don't over-soak them. They make for more comfort and may prevent your hands becoming bruised, which is absolutely essential. If your hands do become bruised you may reach a point where you do not want the ball to come to you and that is a hopeless situation.

Finally, always wear an abdominal protector: it's the common-sense way to avoid a serious injury.

bove: *Agility is one
ssential of wicket-
eeping, as Australia's
n Healy shows against
ngland in 1993.*

ight: *Positioning and
alance are two more.
ngland's Jack Russell is
e role model.*

## Stance

While waiting for the ball to be delivered most keepers place their hands on the ground between their legs, others rest them on their knees and some have their fingers resting on the ground outside their legs.

There is no hard and fast rule; try each position to see which one suits you and adopt the one which feels most comfortable. You may be out in the field for very long periods so comfort is essential. Keep your weight distributed evenly on the balls of both feet so you can move quickly in either direction and try not to tilt your head in order to see the ball. If you look at the ball with your head steady and your eyes level you will focus much better.

## Standing back

Most keepers like to take the ball about waist height and that determines how far back they stand. The aim should be to take a good-length ball just after it begins to drop in its trajectory towards you after pitching.

Position yourself wide of the off stump so you can see the ball all the way from the bowler's hand; don't tuck yourself too far behind the stumps or you will not see balls pitching on the leg stump because of the batsman's body.

A wicket-keeper standing back must always be ready to go for any catch he reckons he can take, boldly and without hesitation. And that applies regardless of the position of the slips.

## Standing up

Most young wicket-keepers feel a bit apprehensive about standing up to the wicket in case the ball is deflected sharply and hits them. That is perfectly understandable but with practice and concentration there is no real need to worry.

Squat down so that your view is not restricted by the batsman's body and keep your head as close to the line of the off stump as possible – the closer the better. Then you will have a good view and be in a position to whip off the bails without stretching or the need for a short pace, which costs valuable time if a stumping chance

David Ripley of Northants has the bails off in a trice against Leicestershire.

Standing up or standing back. Jack Russell shows the concentration of a good keeper who will expect every ball to come through to him.

comes along. Obviously, you should not be so close to the stumps that your movement is restricted by them.

As each delivery rises from the pitch your hands should follow the course of the ball. Never move back from the wicket. If the ball is wide of the stumps move your outside foot sideways to bring head and body across and behind the line.

As soon as you have taken the ball you should be ready to take off the bails. To become a quick stumper you must develop the habit of bringing your hands back towards the wicket after every delivery – even if the batsman has played it. Go through the motions until they become second nature, then you will not have to hurry when a real stumping opportunity occurs.

A wicket-keeper's general attitude and alertness can rub off on the rest of the team. A workmanlike, confident keeper can contribute a great deal to a team's overall performance.

When taking returns from fielders get into position behind the stumps as quickly as possible. Face the fielder and no matter how wild the throw try to take it tidily and before it bounces – never stop it with your pads. If a catch is skied near the wicket, the keeper obviously has a big advantage over other fielders because of his gloves. He should shout 'mine' or preferably 'keeper' so that nobody is left in doubt that he intends to make the catch.

Every wicket-keeper makes mistakes – he is so involved in the play that it would be a miracle if he didn't. But don't dwell on missed chances and let them affect your performance during the rest of the innings. Study the cause later by all means, but try to forget misses once they have happened and concentrate on the next delivery.

Remember, you are looking for reliability and consistency. Sometimes you will produce a really magic moment of which you will be justifiably proud, but there is nothing worse than the keeper who is spectacular and brilliant one day and hopeless the next.

## For the record
Of all players who have scored over 25,000 runs in first-class cricket, Geoff Boycott has the second highest average (after Sir Donald Bradman) – 48,426 runs at 56.83. He scored 151 first-class centuries, which is the fifth highest, and played in 108 Test matches for England, scoring 8,114 runs at 47.72.